Original title:
In the Embrace of Frost

Copyright © 2024 Creative Arts Management OÜ
All rights reserved.

Author: Isabella Rosemont
ISBN HARDBACK: 978-9916-94-620-6
ISBN PAPERBACK: 978-9916-94-621-3

Chilled Hearts and Glimmering Dreams

The snowflakes dance like tiny bugs,
While we sip cocoa and share warm hugs.
A snowman's hat sits crooked and proud,
We laugh at the chaos, oh how loud!

Icicles hang like a frozen choir,
Singing soft tunes that never tire.
We slip on ice, do pirouette spins,
Our winter fun is where joy begins!

The Poetry of Frozen Shadows

Shadows stretch long in the morning light,
They chuckle and giggle, what a funny sight!
A squirrel sings tunes, so off-key and spry,
While freezy breezes make everyone shy.

Snowball fights break the silence around,
With laughter and shrieks, our joy knows no bounds.
Just one little slip, oh what a twist!
It's the giggles of ice that top the list!

A Tapestry of Icy Tranquility

Nature knit blankets, fluffy and white,
Under bright stars that twinkle at night.
With frosty breath we tell silly tales,
Of penguins in suits, riding on whales!

Hot soup steams like a dragon's breath,
As we roast our marshmallows, avoiding the mess.
The cold can't touch us, we dance and we prance,
Life's a big joke, let's all take a chance!

Frosted Lullabies in the Moonlight

Under the moon, the snowflakes hum,
While polar bears tap dance like they're from a drum.
We watch the rabbits hop, oh so bold,
In their tiny sweaters, all fluffy and cold.

Mittens and hats, what a sight to behold,
As we gather 'round, sharing stories untold.
With every snow crunch, our laughter does rise,
Warmed by the joy, 'neath the frosty skies!

A Dance to the Rhythm of Cold

When snowflakes twirl in the blustery air,
A penguin slips, oh such a funny flair!
With wobbly feet, he struggles to stand,
In a chilly ballet across the white land.

Frosty breath paints a mustache of ice,
While kids in mittens attempt to be nice.
Snowballs are flying, laughter's the key,
But watch out for snowmen, they might throw back glee!

The trees wear coats of shimmering white,
The squirrels are gathering, what a silly sight!
They chatter and scamper, all fluffy and round,
Cheeky little bandits in the wintery ground.

So grab your hot cocoa, don't take it too slow,
A dance with the cold is the star of the show!
With giggles and shivers, we conquer the chill,
Embracing the frosty, it brings laughter's thrill.

The Beauty of a Bitter Touch

There's icy art on the windowpanes bright,
With patterns that twinkle like stars in the night.
A snowman tries hard to not lose his hat,
While he's caught in a gust, what a comical spat!

Socks on the floor, you're slipping around,
A puppy is tangled in snow, what a sound!
His tail's a tornado of fluffy white fun,
Chasing after snowflakes, he thinks it's all one!

Wooly scarves dance like they're part of a show,
While mittens go missing—where do they go?
The frozen fingers plot in a giggling spree,
But it's just winter's way of being carefree!

So let's toast to the chill, raising mugs high,
To marshmallows floating like clouds in the sky.
With laughter we conquer each chilly delight,
In the grip of the winter, our spirits take flight.

Captured in a Frost-Kissed Dream

With icicles dangling like silly hats,
The snowman winks, wearing sunglasses and spats.
Frozen squirrels slide down the icy lane,
Chasing snowy snowballs with giggles and gain.

A penguin in boots does a clumsy ballet,
While the frost sparks a dance in a silly way.
Snowflakes giggle, so light in the air,
While snowballs are tossed without any care.

A Dance Among the Winter Shadows

The midnight owls wear a coat of white,
Waltzing in circles, oh what a sight!
Snowflakes spin with a fizz and a pop,
While the frost-covered trees do a frosty hop.

A gopher in mittens strikes a pose,
While snowflakes tickle his little nose.
Chilly winds giggle, whirling around,
Making snow folks tumble and fall to the ground.

Glacial Reflections on a Starlit Night

Stars above twinkle like glittery eyes,
As penguins play chess on the frozen ice!
The moon shares secrets with frosty trees,
While snowflakes dance, caught up in the breeze.

A polar bear juggles with shiny spheres,
Confetti of snowflakes brings joyful cheers.
Glacial mirrors crack with a giggle and snap,
As critters in scarves lay down for a nap.

Haunting Melodies of the Frozen Sky

Ghostly shadows prance on glistening ground,
With icy footsteps, they dance all around.
A waltz with the wind, in a chilly embrace,
While snowmen chuckle, keeping up with the pace.

Frosty notes linger, a whimsical tune,
As the chilly moon peeks out from the gloom.
Trees hum along in a wintery cheer,
Creating a symphony that all critters hear.

Whispers of Winter's Breath

Snowflakes gossip on the ground,
They tickle noses, oh, what a sound!
Penguins sporting tiny hats,
Waddle by, like silly cats.

Icicles are the new cool bling,
What a way to greet the spring!
Frosty breath makes us all laugh,
As snowmen try to do the cha-cha graph.

Slippery sidewalks, a daring thrill,
Watch your steps, or take a spill!
Children skate in frozen shoes,
Not one cares about the blues.

Hot cocoa leads the winter fun,
With extra marshmallows, everyone's won!
Bundled tight, we dance and prance,
While the chill gives a frosty glance.

Echoes of the Crystal Dance

Glistening snow, a crunchy floor,
Squirrels slip and slide, oh what a chore!
Frosty air makes cheeks go red,
While dogs chase tails, full-speed ahead.

Snowball fights erupt with glee,
Some get hit right in the knee!
Laughter echoes through the trees,
As snowflakes swirl like happy bees.

Crisp air whispers cheeky tunes,
While penguins slide beneath the moons.
Everyone's dodging icy blight,
Keeping warm feels just so right.

When winter's antics come to play,
We bundle up and shout hooray!
With every frosty breath we take,
We dance and laugh, for goodness' sake!

Beneath a Shroud of Ice

With ice all around, we play for hours,
Sliding down on makeshift towers.
Frosty breath does bubble and pop,
While giggles rise, they just won't stop.

Snow angels made by flapping arms,
We giggle at their funny charms.
Hot soup's steaming in the pot,
Ice cream's a must, although it's not hot.

Frozen lakes play tricks on us,
Skating fails lead to quite the fuss.
We pick ourselves up from the ground,
And laugh like we've just won a crown!

Chilled to the bone, but spirits are bright,
Snowflakes shimmer like stars at night.
Through winter's mischief, we find delight,
In every frosty laugh, and snowy sight.

Frosty Veils and Silent Nights

The world is draped in a frosty gown,
With giggles echoing all around.
Snowmen pose in the moonlight's glow,
With carrots for noses and eyes aglow.

Winter whispers with frosty breath,
We laugh and cheer, not thinking of death.
Polar bears wear scarves so bright,
Chasing penguins beneath the starlight.

The decorators of snow shovel their way,
While icicles form like the finest ballet.
Snowballs fly, no time for strife,
In this winter wonder, we embrace life.

Frosty nights with candy in hand,
Hot chocolate flowing, tasting so grand.
As we dance under silvery beams,
Winter's humor fuels our dreams.

The Silent Serenade of Snowflakes

Snowflakes dance like clumsy birds,
They twist and twirl without a care.
Landing on noses, toes, and hats,
Tickling cheeks, a chilly dare.

In winter's gown, the world is still,
Yet laughter hides in frozen air.
Each flake a giggle, soft and light,
A frosty joke to make us stare.

With snowy drifts they pile and play,
Creating mounds for us to climb.
We tumble down with squeals of joy,
Nature's humor, a jolly rhyme.

Oh, winter's grip may feel so cold,
But warmth comes from our silly glee.
In frosty winds and playful snow,
We find pure fun in unity.

Embracing the Whispering Chill

Wind whispers secrets, soft and sly,
As scarves and mittens come alive.
The chill might nip, but oh, the fun,
In snowball fights, we laugh and thrive.

Frosty breath dances in the air,
While cheeks turn pink with giddy thrill.
A slippery slide turns kids to gales,
As laughter echoes, joy to spill.

Snowmen sport hats that wobble high,
With crooked smiles, they pose for pics.
But when they melt, oh what a sight,
A puddle left, a joke that clicks.

So hear the chill, with bated breath,
Join in the fun, don't miss the cue.
For in this frost, the laughter glows,
A chilly dance, just me and you.

When Nature Takes a Breath

Nature pauses, takes a breath,
Each snowflake falls, a cheeky jest.
They blank the ground in fluffy coats,
While we sip cocoa, feeling blessed.

Leaves have hidden, trees look bare,
Yet whimsy dances in the frost.
With snowball chuckles flying high,
Don't take it serious; it's a loss.

We skate on lakes of frozen mirth,
As frosty breezes nudge and tease.
The girls and boys with rosy cheeks,
Are swept away by winter's sneeze.

But watch out for that sneaky path,
A slip, a slide, and laughter grows.
We rise again in pure delight,
For winter's just a stage for shows.

Glistening Echoes of the North

Up north, the sun is shy and small,
It glints off snow like diamonds bright.
With every step, the crunch, the snap,
A funny soundtrack, pure delight.

Squirrels in coats of fluffy white,
Chatter with glee, they play around.
While humans bundle, trudge, and slip,
An ice ballet on snowy ground.

Through frosty air, snowflakes swirl,
Tickling noses, teasing chins.
A race to catch them on the tongue,
A winter's challenge: let the fun begin!

So gather round 'neath skies of gray,
With giggles wrapped in winter's cheer.
For through the frost, the joy will bloom,
In every chilly, chuckling year.

Frosted Leaves and Winter's Breath

Chilled leaves giggle on the ground,
Tickled by whispers all around.
Squirrels don coats, fashionably brown,
While snowmen grin in a frozen town.

Faces bright with snowy glee,
In the cold, they dance with ease.
Hot cocoa spills, oh what a sight!
Rounding up snowballs for a snowball fight.

Puddles freeze into slick delights,
Slipping here, oh what funny sights!
Jumping jacks in thermal shorts,
As frosty air makes silly snorts.

Carrots stuck on icy heads,
Frosted jokes keep us in our beds.
Winter wraps us in a hug,
And laughter's warmth gives us a shrug.

Threads of Ice in the Twilight

Icicles dangle like silly hats,
On rooftops where the chilly bat.
Sneaky snowflakes take a dive,
As we all try to survive.

Noses red from frosty kisses,
Children make snow angels in misses.
Winter's breath is a sugar rush,
Joyful chaos in every hush.

Mittens on, but one is lost,
Laughter echoes, what a cost!
Frosty friends in the twilight glow,
With jolly hearts, off they go.

Sliding down hills like a pro,
Cheeks aglow in the winter's show.
Woolly hats and boots abound,
In this twilight, joy is found!

Hushed Secrets of the Winter Night

Whispering winds tell tales anew,
Of snowflakes giggling as they flew.
Mittens misplaced, lost without a care,
Dashing through snow drifts, unaware.

Rabbits dressed in winter gear,
Bounce around with cheerful cheer.
Frosted whispers fill the air,
While squirrels plot winter's dare.

Snowball battles spark delight,
As friends gather on winter's night.
Snowmen wobbly, needing a snack,
With buttons falling, there's no turning back.

Starlit skies are a frosty treat,
Where laughter blends with icy sweet.
Secrets chill, but spirits warm,
In the night, we weather the storm.

Tapestry of Snowflakes

Snowflakes dance like tiny stars,
Falling down from velvet jars.
With each flake, a giggle rolls,
Covering all of winter's trolls.

Frosted lawns are merry sights,
Where children dash in fuzzy tights.
They tumble and roll, laughter ignites,
Creating joy in bundle bites.

Candy canes in the frosty chill,
While shadows play on the window sill.
Frosty breath sends puffs in the air,
With snowy mischief everywhere!

Icicles hang like frozen glee,
And snowmen dance like they're carefree.
In this tapestry, bright and sweet,
Winter's humor can't be beat!

Frost-Kissed Memories

Snowflakes land on my nose,
I sneeze and scare a crow.
A penguin slips on banana peels,
Ice skating? Not for me, though.

Socks and mittens are mismatched,
My mittens look like a clown.
But frosty breath is quite a sight,
When the sun is sliding down.

Snowman grins with a carrot nose,
Wobbles in the breeze.
I toss a snowball, it backfires,
And I'm covered like a cheese.

Chilled air lifts my spirits high,
Winter's quirks keep me amused.
In this wonderland of giggles,
I laugh until I'm bruised.

The Quiet Dance of Ice

The icy pond holds a secret,
Ready for a slip and slide.
But as I glide, I twist and twirl,
And make my backside my pride.

Dancing with frozen fish below,
They think it's quite a show.
An audience of chilly trees,
Who twitch with every toe.

Icicles hang like chandeliers,
While squirrels bound in glee.
They think they're the stars of the day,
But really, it's just me!

With frosty curls and rosy cheeks,
I laugh 'til my sides are sore.
In this icy waltz of winter,
I slip and flop evermore!

Glistening Shadows of December

The moon shines bright on frozen lakes,
Where shadows dance and prance.
But when I join that icy jig,
My feet forget the chance.

I leap and land in fluffy snow,
With every roll, I giggle.
A snow angel flops and flails,
Winter's daring wiggle.

My cheeks match the nose of Rudolph,
Red as cherries in a pie.
I wonder if the frost can melt,
With every silly sigh.

Glistening grains of ice and grit,
Tickle toes and winter dreams.
Warming up with cups of cocoa,
While plotting snowball schemes.

Bound by the Frigid Touch

In a land where the snowflakes prank,
    I trip over an unseen prank.
Every winter groove I take,
    Feels like a wobbly plank.

Snowmen plotting winter schemes,
    Conspire with the frost.
With carrot noses pointing me,
    I'm never really lost.

As frostbite tries to steal my toes,
    I giggle and jump around.
Chasing shadows of playful clouds,
    That scatter on frozen ground.

With every shiver and every twirl,
    Joy dances in the cold.
This frosty place brings out the child,
    In winter's funny fold.

Heartbeats in the Chill

The snowflakes dance, they twirl in glee,
They land on my nose, oh look at me!
With icy breaths and frozen hair,
I joke with squirrels, they don't seem to care.

My fingers numb, they wave around,
I try to catch a snowman, but fall to the ground!
A chilly grin, as I slip on ice,
The world laughs aloud, oh what a heist!

I built a fort, but it fell apart,
With every gust, it stole my heart.
A snowball battle, I launch with might,
They hit me back, oh what a fright!

But through the frosty, chilly games,
Laughter echoes, no one blames.
In winter's grip, we're all just fools,
Sledding down hills, breaking all the rules!

Whispering Pines in White

The pines are dressed in white and fluff,
They whisper secrets, but it's all too tough!
I asked the trees, they just nodded slow,
Guess they know more than me, oh no!

Snowmen standing, with corncob pipes,
Fashion disasters, those quirky types!
With carrot noses and hats askew,
They wave at the rabbits, saying, "Howdy-doo!"

The squirrels are bustling, preparing a feast,
But keep dropping acorns, oh what a beast!
I slip on a branch, land face-first in snow,
The pines just chuckle, they don't let it go!

The air is crisp, the skies a bright gray,
While I ponder life in this frosty ballet.
My winter tale, a comedy scene,
Dancing through snowflakes, all in between!

When Time Stopped in Silver

A silver blanket covers the ground,
In this winter wonder, no time's around.
I tried to walk, but my feet got cold,
Froze on the spot, oh what a hold!

A chipmunk stared, gave me a wink,
While I pondered if snowflakes could drink.
With icicles hanging from every tree,
I asked a snowman, "Would you care for tea?"

Hours passed, or maybe just a minute,
With snowballs flying, I just can't win it.
I called for help, but no one would hear,
Only a snowdog gave me a cheer.

As daylight fades, the stars come out,
The snow says, "Shush!" while whirling about.
I tiptoe carefully, feeling quite spry,
When I'm stuck like this, who really knows why?

Constellations of Frozen Tears

The night is bright, but freezing too,
Stars twinkle above, a dazzling view.
Yet tears freeze up as I look 'round,
Am I laughing or lost? Not quite sure, I've found.

A dog barks once, then chases its tail,
I laugh so hard, it's starting to hail!
Puddles of snow, splatters on my face,
A frosty rendezvous, an awkward grace.

The stars seem to wink, full of delight,
As I tumble and roll, yielding to fright.
Through frozen laughter, I slip with glee,
Making snow angels, for the world to see!

In this winter scene, I dance and play,
A little humor goes a long way.
So let the frost cover all with cheer,
For laughter warms even the coldest year!

Crystal Wings of the Cold

Snowflakes dance like happy fleas,
Chasing dreams on winter's breeze.
They tickle noses, playfully tease,
Wishing all to freeze with ease.

Icicles hang like crooked teeth,
A mouth wide-open, 'neath the sheath.
They glare down with a frosty wreath,
As if saying, "Chill out, don't be a heath!"

Frosty boots and mittens worn,
Slide on ice like kids, all torn.
We stumble laugh, look quite forlorn,
The winter joy, we've gladly sworn.

Snowmen strike a goofy pose,
With carrot noses, fashion shows.
They wave to all as they decompose,
A winter fashion no one knows!

Echoes of the Freezing Moon

The moon's a disco ball of chill,
It sparkles high on every hill.
While raccoons search for a winter thrill,
Wearing scarves, they dance, what a skill.

Breezes whisper, "Bundle up tight!"
As squirrels leap in a snowy bite.
They chitter tricks in frosty light,
With little hats, oh what a sight!

Puddles freeze like glassy ponds,
Reflections tease with winter's fronds.
We skate and slip, a chorus responds,
With laughter echoing like magic wands.

Hot cocoa warms our frozen hands,
As we recount our snowy plans.
Winter's here with all its demands,
But in our hearts, we make our stands!

Shards of Winter's Lament

In a park, a snowball fight,
Kids giggle, oh what a sight!
But one runs into a tree with fright,
Leaves behind a frosty blight.

The dogs in sweaters, snug and proud,
Bark at snowflakes—oh how loud!
Chasing tails in a frigid crowd,
They twirl around, as if they're cowed.

Snow gets tracked inside the house,
A mountain left for cat and mouse.
Mittens vanish, oh, what a douse!
The day ends with a frosty rouse.

Grandma's soup brings joy anew,
Sipping warmth like a winter stew.
We laugh at all the chaos blue,
In this frosty world, it's never through!

The Breath of a Frozen Dawn

Morning light with icy breath,
Paints the world as if from death.
While boots squeak like a choir's meth,
The air is crisp, we take a heft.

Dogs slide by on icy paws,
Chasing light without a cause.
They leap and stink at phantom flaws,
While we giggle at their claws.

Hot air balloons, the coffee kind,
Puff up cheer as we unwind.
With marshmallows floating, eyes aligned,
The joy of warmth, forever twined.

So let's embrace this frosty morn,
With cups held high, our spirits born.
In laughter's glow, we'll never mourn,
For winter's charm is never worn!

Crystalized Moments of Silence

Snowflakes dance on my nose,
Chilling me down to my toes.
I slip on ice, oh what a sight,
Giggling snowmen join the fight.

Hot cocoa laughs in my mug,
Marshmallows bob like a snug bug.
My scarf's a magical mess,
Even penguins would say, 'God bless!'

Snowball fights, who's throwing right?
Laughter echoes, pure delight.
But alas, I trip, oh dear me,
I'm now the star of this snow spree!

Frosty breath with a chirpy sound,
Chasing snowflakes that twirl around.
Winter woes turned into glee,
Each slip's a win, it seems to be!

The Artistry of Silvered Woods

Trees stand tall with frosty hair,
Whispering secrets in the cold air.
Critters giggle, all tucked tight,
As squirrels bumble, what a sight!

Pine cones launch, a playful game,
Playing tag, they're so the same.
Branches creak, a subtle joke,
Nature's laugh, oh how it woke!

Icicles hang like pointed hats,
Winking down at little rats.
The woods are dressed in silver lace,
Even the snowmen join the race!

Winter spreads her chilly cheer,
While I wrap up, shedding a tear.
The beauty's here, but so's my sneeze,
Nature chuckles with such ease!

Winter's Shimmering Canvas

A canvas spread, all white and bright,
Puppies tumble, pure delight.
Their paws paint tales of playful glee,
Chasing shadows, wild, and free.

Snowballs gather, soft and round,
Flying fast, oh, what a sound!
Yet there's one who takes a dive,
And joins the snow with a joyful jive!

The squirrels gather for a show,
Chasing tails while I throw snow.
Twinkling lights on frosted trees,
Nature herself joins us with ease!

Laughter echoes through the air,
As carolers sing without a care.
Winter's brush strokes laughs so grand,
Artistry made by nature's hand!

Frosted Wishes in the Air

Wishing on a snowflake's fall,
Caught in a tizzy, I'm having a ball!
A slip, a slide, oh, watch out there!
Frosted wishes float everywhere!

Snowmen smile with button eyes,
As snowflakes twirl like tiny spies.
They laugh and prance in soft white gear,
While I yell out, "I volunteer!"

Hot chocolate spills, a bubbling cheer,
Marshmallows float, they persevere.
Sipping slowly, I count each sip,
As winter's frolic makes me slip!

Jingle bells in the frosty air,
With every slip, I lose my care.
Each frosted wish, both here and there,
Winter giggles, a cold affair!

The Stillness of Frosted Dawn

When morning breaks and chill is keen,
The world is draped in sparkling sheen.
A squirrel slips on ice so slick,
While birds wear coats, oh what a trick!

The trees stand tall, their limbs astound,
Like dancers frozen, still they're found.
A rabbit hops with style and flair,
Then slips and tumbles without a care.

The sun peeks out, a grin so wide,
The frost fairies giggle, wanting to hide.
One throws a snowball, laughter in air,
Nature's own circus, beyond compare!

So bundle up, let jokes unfold,
In frosty fun, let tales be told.
With every slip and slide we glee,
A winter's joke, come laugh with me!

Nature's Pale Embrace

Snowflakes dance and frolic around,
While trees wear white, oh what a crown!
A penguin waddle makes me cheer,
As frosty critters shout, "Winter's here!"

The pond looks like a giant plate,
Where ducks slide in, they call it fate.
They wear ice skates, oh so chic,
In penguin style, it's quite the peak!

A snowman grins with carrot nose,
To everyone's joy, he strikes a pose.
But when the sun beams down so bright,
He melts away, oh what a sight!

So raise a glass of cocoa warm,
To nature's charm, its quirky norm.
For laughter lingers in the air,
In cold's embrace, we share the flare!

Waking Dreams of a Snowbound World

In slumber deep, the world does dream,
Of fluffy pillows, a snowy theme.
A cat in boots takes on the snow,
With paws in clumps, oh what a show!

Kids on sleds, whoosh, away they fly,
While grumpy grandpa lets out a sigh.
He slips and lands with a comedic thud,
Snowflakes landing like a subtle flood.

The snowmen gather for a chat,
"Who wore a hat? Was it you, or that?"
They gossip on the icy route,
While frosty wind gives them a pout.

Their noses red, a joyful sight,
A world wrapped up in pure delight.
So toast the fun on winter's stage,
In waking dreams, let joy engage!

The Secret Life of Frost

When night descends with twinkling stars,
The frost creeps in with little cars.
Tiny critters zoom along,
With icy tires, they sing their song!

The otter installs a winter slide,
While the owl hoots, he's full of pride.
The bunnies play a game of chase,
Sliding by in a frosty race.

With every sparkle, laughter roars,
Together they open winter's doors.
A snowman, bossy, says, "Let's fight!"
But everyone giggles; it's just their night.

As dawn breaks warm and sunlight's near,
The frost's gone home, it leaves a cheer.
But in the shadows, a game's reborn,
For frosty fun will always adorn!

The Still Air of Snowy Dawn

The snowflakes fall with quite a flair,
Dancing around like they just don't care.
The squirrels are slipping, oh what a sight,
Chasing their tails in morning light.

Penguins in coats that look out of style,
Waddle along with a charming smile.
Hot cocoa spills on the ground with glee,
"Punxsutawney Phil, what have you seen?"

Chattering birds in winter's chill,
Gossip about the snowman's skill.
"Too much carrot, he looks quite round!"
Yet still they laugh without a sound.

The world is dressed in icy cheer,
Mittens on hands bring warmth and cheer.
Snowball fights break out, what a mess,
Ending with snowflakes on each dress.

Dusk Beneath the Frosted Boughs

The trees wear blankets of sparkling white,
While rabbits hop into the night.
They nibble carrots, they munch and munch,
While dreaming of a very big brunch.

A hoot from the owl, a scream from the crow,
Who wore their best coats, but still felt low.
"Is winter always this cold?" they complain,
"Next year, a trip to the beach, that's our gain!"

The moon giggles down at the ground below,
As snowflakes tickle the frogs in a show.
A kazoo band forms under the trees,
Playing tunes that float in the freeze.

Up jumps a penguin to join the fun,
"Where do I fit in?" shouts a raccoon run.
They jive and wiggle, what a sight,
As frost paints all in silver delight.

Timeless Echoes of Glittering Frost

The rooftops glimmer like diamonds on fire,
While snowplows go by with an honest tire.
A googly-eyed snowman takes a short break,
To sip hot chocolate, make no mistake!

A gathering of folks in woolly hats,
Debating if snowmen really are brats.
But every snowflake knows it's just a game,
"Let's toss a few, and not feel the shame!"

Feet slip and slide on the icy ground,
While laughter echoes, all round and round.
Then someone tumbles, arms in the air,
"Send help!" they cry, "I'm stuck in despair!"

The night grows quiet, a blanket of hush,
Yet giggles still bubble in a friendly rush.
As frost sings songs of the jolly old days,
Who knew winter could come in such playful ways?

Frosted Paths and Silent Journeys

The path is frosty, a glittery bread,
With every step, old tales are read.
Carrots parade on the way to the feast,
While bunnies hop happily, not the least.

Snowflakes whisper secrets as they fall,
Unbothered by squirrels doing a crawl.
"Did you hear the one about a snowball fight?
Count your throws, or you'll lose your might!"

The moon dips low, casting shadows so sleek,
While penguins gather to have a little peek.
With a flipper raised, they all take a bow,
"Let's waddle and dance, right here, right now!"

Footprints linger like giggles in air,
Leading to places without a care.
With each little step, the cold feels less,
In a world where laughter's the warmest dress.

The Chill of Solitude's Embrace

When snowflakes dance on lonely streets,
   I wear my scarf like a giant sheet.
The silence whispers with frosty cheer,
   I swear I heard a snowman sneer.

My coffee's cold, my toes are numb,
I chase the warmth, but it's so dumb.
Wrapped in blankets, I ponder life,
Should I go out? Nah, not worth the strife.

Each breath a cloud, each laugh a fight,
   Winter seems to think it's so polite.
But I can see through the chilly plot,
   There's mischief hiding in every spot.

In this frozen funk that feels so grand,
I think I'll take up ice sculpting, planned!
But with my luck, it'd surely melt,
   Leaving behind the cold I felt.

Frost-Laden Dreams in the Night

I dream of penguins in their tuxedos,
Sliding through snow on tiny speedos.
Their frosty waddle, a comical sight,
 I laugh too hard, oh what a night!

As I sip cocoa, a fluffy delight,
My cat plots mischief, he's out of sight.
He leaps for the curtains, a daring heist,
 Only to land in a bowl of ice.

The chill outside tells tales of jest,
Where every snowball is put to the test.
The neighbors yell, "Watch out, you fool!"
But I'm too busy making snow angels drool.

Frosty dreams have us all bemused,
In this frosted wonder, I feel amused.
Tomorrow's chill will bring more fun,
Catch me outside—oh wait, I'm done!

A Tinge of Ice on the Soul

Ice cubes jingle in my drink so cold,
My heart feels frosty, or so I'm told.
I wear my mittens, they're too snug,
But with every sip, I feel more smug.

The snowman laughs as I slosh around,
It seems he's got the upper ground.
His carrot nose, so proud and bright,
Mocks my winter fashion, what a sight!

A sled ride stirs both joy and dread,
With every bump, I think I'm dead.
The ice is slick, my pants are wet,
A graceful fall? Not one I'd bet.

But through the cold and icy strife,
I find the warmth in this winter life.
With friends beside me, we'll share a cheer,
Even if it's frozen, oh dear!

Shards of Winter's Light

The sun peeks through with frosty rays,
While I'm still dreaming in a snowy haze.
I try to build a gingerbread house,
But end up crafting a snowman mouse!

My cat, a furry winter fiend,
Chases snowflakes like they're mean.
He swats them down with a pounce and turn,
While from the ground, I laugh and burn.

Sledding feels like a turbulent ride,
With laughter echoing as I glide.
Face-first in snow, I plop and roll,
A chilling experience, warms my soul.

So here's to frosty times and glee,
A little humor, wild and free.
With every ice patch, we slip and fall,
Winter's punchline is the best of all.

Twilight's Frosty Caress

The snowflakes dance and spin around,
As penguins wobble on icy ground.
A snowman sneezes, what a sight,
With carrot nose, he took a bite!

The chill tickles my nose just so,
I wear my beanie, it's all aglow.
With mittens mismatched, I'm quite the sight,
Trying to sled and putting up a fight!

Icicles dangle, sharp and long,
They hum a tune like a winter song.
But one falls down with a mighty thud,
And lands right in my hot cocoa mug!

The winter winds begin to howl,
As squirrels plot their snowy prowl.
Yet here I stand, a frozen grin,
Wishing somehow for spring to win!

The Stillness of Winter's Heart

Outside it glimmers, the world so white,
But I found my sock—it's quite a fright!
The left one's missing, oh what a fail,
Did it vanish like the snow in a hail?

The trees wear blankets, fluffy and wide,
While I trip over my own two feet in stride.
A polar bear laughs as he slides, too,
On a melt-in-your-mouth chocolate fondue!

Snowflakes fall like confetti, hooray!
They tickle my chin and lead me astray.
With every step, a slip and a slide,
The laughter builds as I kiss the ice wide!

But hot chocolate waits with marshmallows fair,
My snowy mischief will lead me there.
With cheeks all rosy and laughter loud,
Winter's chill can't melt my spirit proud!

Surrendering to the Glacial Stillness

Slippery sidewalks greet my shoe,
How did I land on my back? Who knew?
With a puff of snow upon my head,
I chuckle and wish for a warmer bed.

Snow angels made in a hurry and haste,
With every flail, it's a snowy race!
But when I stand, oh what a sight,
A lopsided angel, quite the plight!

The air is crisp, I wheeze and whine,
As I find my nose has lost its shine.
A snowball toss goes completely wrong,
I hit the cat, it gives a yowl song!

Yet here we are in the frosty glow,
Sharing laughter amidst the snow.
With friends beside in a wintry spree,
Life's just better with frosty glee!

Frostbitten Reveries

The winter sun peeks through the frost,
While my patience melts like my toes, I'm lost.
A penguin steals my scarf, oh dear,
Wiggling away with a joyful cheer!

The snowdrifts giggle as we tread,
Right into a snowball fight instead!
Catching snowflakes on eager tongues,
We sing out loud, our weird winter songs.

My breath makes clouds that dance and spin,
But the cat leaps out, oh where to begin?
She pounces on snow with a triumphant leap,
I trip over her, in a pile, we heap!

Yet, as daylight wanes, we gather near,
With cocoa so sweet, we have no fear.
For frosty times can warm the heart,
Especially when laughter plays its part!

The Timekeeper of Frozen Moments

A snowman checks the time, you see,
With a carrot nose, he glances with glee.
His watch is made of ice and dreams,
Sipping cocoa, or so it seems.

When the clock strikes twelve, he'll take a dance,
Twisting and turning in his frozen stance.
His hat is tilted, his buttons askew,
Mismatched mittens in colors so blue.

He giggles as he melts, just a tad,
'What a party!' he shouts, 'I'm not really bad!'
With every warm sunbeam that drifts on by,
He swirls into laughter, then waves goodbye.

So cherish the frosty, the silly, the sweet,
In every chilly moment, there's joy to greet!
For time does freeze in the most curious ways,
With a snowman's chuckles to brighten our days!

Reflecting the Chill of Twilight

Under the glow of a frosty moon,
Dancing snowflakes hum a silly tune.
Icicles hang like teetering toys,
See them shimmer and almost make noise!

Beneath the chill, two penguins play,
Skating on ponds till the break of day.
With flippers flailing and hats upon heads,
They giggle and tumble, making their beds.

The stars above wear frosty crowns,
While laughter echoes through snowy towns.
A rabbit trips over his own big feet,
Rolling in laughter, he can't feel the heat!

As twilight lingers, stars wipe their tears,
Of joy and laughter across the years.
Frosty spirits dance, oh what a sight,
Celebrating the chill with sheer delight!

Frigid Hues and Blushing Stars

The colors fly in the winter night,
With oranges and pinks that feel just right.
Snowflakes paint the town with flair,
While giggling squirrels twirl in the air.

A star falls down, with a cheeky grin,
'This frost is cozy, let's all jump in!'
It bounces on ice, spinning like mad,
Causing all who see it to feel quite glad.

Pajama-clad kids launch snowball fights,
As the moonlight glimmers with playful lights.
They stumble and fall, all giggles and cheer,
With frosty whispers that draw everyone near.

So breathe in the cold with a laugh and a jig,
For winter's just a big, fluffy gig!
In colors so bright and hearts full of cheer,
These moments of frost will keep us all near!

A Gilded Touch of the Icy Hand

A frosty breath tickles the trees,
Each branch wearing coats of icy freeze.
A snowflake lands with a dancey prance,
Winking at the world, oh what a chance!

The chilly winds whistle a cheeky tune,
While birds burrow deep, avoiding the moon.
One little chick peeks out with a shout,
'Is the coast clear? I'm ready to pout!'

Oh, the laughter that spills from lips so bright,
As we frolic in wonder, not fearing the night.
With each bite of cocoa and snuggle so tight,
Ice can't freeze the joy we hold at night!

So let's wrap ourselves in furs so warm,
And dance in the snow, oh isn't it charm?
For each glittery moment that graces our way,
Brings laughter and cheer, come what may!

The Dreamscape of Winter's Embrace

Chilling winds whisper tales to the trees,
Socks on the line, flapping like fleas.
Snowmen grinning with carrot nose flair,
Beware of the snowball fight in the air!

Hot cocoa spills, oh what a mess,
Marshmallows float like a jolly dress.
Slippers slide, like penguins on ice,
Who knew our backyard could be so nice?

Snowflakes tumble, giggling around,
Dressed like sprinkles, they dance on the ground.
Except for that one that got stuck on my nose,
It sneezed, and then BOOM! The whole world froze!

Icicles dangling like shiny spears,
They capture my breath with frostbite cheers.
We waddle and slip down the snowy slope,
Laughing so hard, we might just elope!

Frosted Glimmer in the Stillness

Morning frost makes everything gleam,
Shiny and bright, it's the perfect scheme.
But oh! That patch where the snow leopards tread,
Turns out to be where my dog just sped!

Gloves lost in the depths of the yard,
Searching for matches can be quite hard.
Oh, the hand warmers staged a revolt,
Now they're just rocks, it's my fault or the cold's fault?

Scarves tangled like pretzels in the wind,
A face full of snow, on that I depend.
Fuzzy hats bobbing, a fashion delight,
We strut our stuff, it's a winter's fight!

Sunshine peeks in, a welcome guest,
Melting our faces, it's nature's jest.
Frosted glimmers, slipping around,
It's hard to keep laughter from leaving this ground!

An Icy Canvas of Dreams

The world's turned white, oh what a sight,
Sleds dashed by in sheer delight.
Wipeouts occur in synchronized glee,
Slipping and sliding, just like me!

Carrots for noses, hats all askew,
Snowmen chat under skies so blue.
Oh wait, that's just my buddy Fred,
He's had too much cocoa, and now he's red!

Footprints mar the perfect white space,
Who knew winter could be such a race?
With each tiny flake, a giggle does bloom,
Especially when penguins invade the room!

Twinkling lights on the house so fine,
Winter's a party, check out that line!
Hot pies are cooling – shhh, do not shout,
That's Grandma's, and we don't want a pout!

When Snowflakes Weave Their Tales

Snowflakes tumble, oh what a spree,
Whirling around, they laugh and flee.
But in the middle of this frosty ballet,
My boots gained a mind of their own today!

Sliding and crashing like a comet's fall,
I wish I could use magic – or a wall.
From 'elegant dancer' to 'flailing kite',
My snow-filled dreams are now quite a sight.

Fortresses built, oh what a thrill,
But they crumble faster than I can fill.
A snowball rolls that gives quite a scare,
Now it's chasing me, oh – where's the fair?

Hot cocoa awaits, a warm little hug,
But first, my nose needs a friendly rug.
Winter's bright palette makes me all giddy,
Especially when snowball fights get all gritty!

Whispers of Snow Beyond the Mountains

Snowflakes dance and twirl in flight,
Chasing squirrels, what a sight!
They land on noses, hats, and cars,
As we laugh underneath the stars.

Frosty breath like dragons puff,
Making us think we're super tough,
But slip on ice, oh what a game,
We all squeal, but who's to blame?

Snowmen sporting hats askew,
With carrot noses peeking through,
They stand as guards till springtime's call,
Who knew they'd have a grand snowball?

As flakes tickle our chilly cheeks,
We're childlike, finding smiles in weeks,
In nature's freeze, we find such cheer,
With frosty giggles ringing clear.

The Beauty of a Frozen Solstice

The sun takes naps, oh what a tease,
While icicles hang from freezing trees,
We bundle up in layers thick,
And hope we don't end up in a lick!

Eggnog spills on frosted ground,
And laughter spreads all around,
Warmed by fluff and quirky hats,
We slip and slide like clumsy cats.

Carols echo through the air,
While snowmen sport a silly stare,
With buttons mismatched, and scarves too loose,
They giggle at their own excuse.

The cold may bite, but joy won't freeze,
As we gather, friends with ease,
In this frosty wonderland's hold,
Funny stories waiting to be told.

Solace Found in Winter's Spell

Hot cocoa spills, oh what a mess,
Making our fingers feel the stress,
We peer outside at snowflakes' flight,
And wonder if they've got a flight!

Sleds that tumble down the hill,
Demanding laughter shared until,
We crash in powder, hats askew,
Our giggles float like dreams anew.

Frosty noses, cheeks aglow,
As we chase each other, to and fro,
In winter games, we claim our space,
While snowflakes dance in joyful grace.

Chasing shadows in the night,
Slipping and sliding, such delight,
In this chill, our hearts will swell,
Finding warmth in winter's spell.

Frosted Reflections in the Dark

Under the moon, the snow does gleam,
Like a giant marshmallow dream,
We tiptoe softly, quiet and bright,
Look out for yetis, 'cause they bite!

Biting cold and laughter roars,
While mittens flutter like open doors,
A snowball flies! Did it hit you?
Face the frosty war — it's true!

Snowflakes falling, swirling fast,
Catching wishes, what a blast,
Dreams dance by in cozy socks,
As winter's comedy unlocks.

In frosty mirrors, we all see,
The humor in our shuffling spree,
In cold embrace, we find our spark,
Together laughing—what a lark!

Frost's Gentle Touch on the World

Frost tickles rooftops, a chilly tease,
As dogs in sweaters trip over leaves.
Snowflakes dance like a jolly crew,
Sleds turn sideways; oh, what a view!

Icicles hang like sharp silver spears,
While snowmen giggle, hiding their fears.
Sneaky squirrels bury nuts in their haste,
Winter's playground, no time to waste.

Boots get stuck in mushy, wet snow,
As kids scream loudly, "Look out below!"
Hot cocoa spills, marshmallows fly,
In frosty fun, we laugh and sigh.

Oh, the chill brings a frosty cheer,
With every slip, we shed a tear.
Winter's grip, a frolicsome sight,
Under the stars, everything's bright!

The Secrets of Winter's Cloak

When winter comes with her fluffy gown,
She wraps the world in white satin down.
Birds wear socks, or so it seems,
Chirping loudly, living their dreams.

The subtle crunch beneath my feet,
Makes me feel like a clumsy sleet.
Snowflakes laugh as they fall and glide,
Making me tumble, twist, and slide.

Snowball fights lead to shrieks and glee,
As mom yells, "Come in! No more debris!"
Winter's secrets, hidden quite well,
Are shared in giggles, like tales to tell.

Frosty mornings are truly a gift,
With every fall, heightening the rift.
In the cloak of winter, we all find joy,
A playful chill for every girl and boy!

Magic Woven in Ice

A snowy landscape, a sight so fine,
Frogs in the pond do the winter's line.
They hop on skates, who knew they could?
A chorus of laughs, oh, isn't it good?

The trees wear coats, all sparkling bright,
As chipmunks join in a dance at night.
A puddle froze, now a disco ball,
Winter's magic, we're having a ball!

Rabbits in mittens, such a silly sight,
Dancing in circles, what a delight!
Snowflakes whisper secrets on their way,
Inviting us all for a joyful play.

In ice castles made of glimmering light,
We giggle and prance, hearts feeling so light.
So let's embrace this quirky cold song,
For in winter's charm, we all belong!

An Ode to the Whispering Wind

Oh whispering wind, with your icy breath,
You poke at my nose, challenging death.
Turning my cheeks into rosy hue,
You tease and you taunt; what's a girl to do?

Under your guidance, the snowflakes sway,
Leading a parade in their frosty ballet.
I chase after clouds with chores in tow,
But each gust reminds me to take it slow.

The trees lean in, as your shriek grows loud,
Wishing for silence from the giggling crowd.
But I can't complain, for you bring such cheer,
Turning dull days into bold laughter here.

So here's to the wind, so playful and free,
With every gust and shiver, we feel so carefree.
Together with snow, you create quite the show,
In this winterland, let the funny winds blow!

Chill of Winter's Whisper

Snowflakes dance, a playful flight,
Hiding from snowmen, in sheer delight.
I think they're plotting, to tickle my nose,
With frozen fingers, that nobody knows.

Ice on the window, a frosty art,
My breath fogs the glass, a fine winter's start.
Hot cocoa bubbles, it's time for a sip,
But the marshmallows wobble, and threaten to flip.

Sledding down hills, like a bird with no wings,
I'm laughing so hard, oh the joy that it brings.
But watch out for trees, they can ruin your cheer,
As winter giggles, loud and near.

Furry friends snuggle, wrapped up so tight,
Chasing their tails, what a silly sight!

Veils of Icy Elegance

Icicles hanging like fancy décor,
I slip on the sidewalk, then laugh on the floor.
Fashioned by frost, in this wintery scene,
My style's never better, or so it would seem.

Snowflakes like glitter, a dazzling show,
While I search for boots, with a fashionable glow.
The hat's on sideways, I'm sporting a style,
Of "I just woke up," with a snow-covered smile.

Squirrels in jackets, with attitude bold,
Stealing my birdseed, like treasures of gold.
But I laugh at their antics, as they stuff and they munch,
And winter winks back, as I sip my warm brunch.

With laughter and warmth in every cold breath,
I embrace this chill, like it's life or death.
Each frosty adventure, a giggle parade,
In veils of iciness, my joy won't fade.

Frosted Dreams Awaken

Morning light creeps, the landscape aglow,
While I snooze on in dreams, all wrapped up in woe.
The sun's giggling loudly, 'Time to get up!'
But I roll on my side, 'Just one more cup!'

Pancakes are flipping, the syrup's a treat,
But snow on the porch makes me shuffle my feet.
The mailman's out there, a bundle of cheer,
But I hide behind curtains, hoping he'll clear.

Winter's a joker, with a snowball to throw,
I duck and I dodge, laughing high with the snow.
The world spins in white, a whimsical thrill,
With frosted dreams waking, I have time to kill.

So join in the laughter, as we prance in the chill,
With each icy breath, let's savor the thrill.
Giggles and snowflakes, a delightful embrace,
In this chilly kingdom, we'll find our own pace.

Silence Beneath the Snow

A hush on the world, soft blankets unfold,
Underneath it all, the stories are told.
The squirrels are plotting their next big heist,
As I sip on my cocoa, I can't help but be nice.

The trees stand so still, dressed in their white,
Whispers of winter laugh softly at night.
"Check out these snowflakes!" I shout with delight,
But they twirl and they dance, then vanish from sight.

Frost nips my nose, and I giggle aloud,
As I trip on a twig, my fate's oh so proud.
The laughter of children echoes up high,
While snowballs zip by like a mischievous spy.

In this wintry silence, there's chaos, it's true,
Where frost plays a symphony, just for me and you.
So let's wrap up this season with laughter and cheer,
With smiles in the snow, it's the best time of year.

Celestial Ice and Ethereal Light

Snowflakes twirl like tiny sprites,
While snowmen grin with carrot bites.
The trees wear coats of shimmering white,
As squirrels slide in sheer delight.

Hot cocoa spills, a comical splash,
As mittens disappear, oh what a crash!
The frozen pond becomes a slide,
With laughter echoing far and wide.

Frosty mornings bring playful schemes,
While boots stomp loudly in winter dreams.
The sun peeks out, a warm surprise,
As snowflakes sparkle like mischievous eyes.

Under the moon, the world's so bright,
As snowmen dance in the pale moonlight.
With every sip of cheer and glee,
Winter's charm is wild and free.

The Enchantment of Winter's Grasp

Icicles hang like nature's teeth,
As snowflakes waltz in a frosty sheath.
The rabbits hop with silly grace,
While winter's chill plays tag, a race.

People slip and take a tumble,
As snowballs fly, and giggles rumble.
Frosty faces, rosy and bright,
Pretending we're all in a snowball fight.

Woolly hats askew on heads,
While snowmen snooze in their frosty beds.
The chill brings out the jolly cheer,
Each frosty breath whispers holiday near.

With every snow drift, surprises loom,
As we carve angels in winter's room.
The enchantment wraps us oh so tight,
In a whirlwind of laughter, pure delight.

Veils of Crystal Dreams

Frosty whispers weave through the trees,
Like giggles shared with a chilly breeze.
Snow blankets hide all but the fun,
Where laughter glimmers like a bright morning sun.

Chubby snowflakes bounce on the ground,
As the world dons a blanket, feathered and round.
The dog leaps high in joyful arcs,
Chasing snowballs, leaving silly marks.

Hot soup spills in a clumsy pour,
As mittens warm up by the stove's core.
Snowmen's noses get slightly askew,
With each playful gust that blows right through.

Let's twirl and twirl till we fall in a heap,
While the icy wind sings us to sleep.
Veils of white swirl, twinkling bright,
In this funny dance of pure winter's light.

Dances with the Winter Muse

Winter's breezes bring silly cheer,
As frosty pixies gossip near.
With every step, the ground does squeak,
As laughter bubbles; it's joy we seek.

Giggling gusts can play a prank,
As hats fly off and tumble, swank!
Snowflakes stick to noses bright,
A frosty masterpiece, pure delight.

In cozy boots, we stomp around,
Creating patterns on the ground.
A snowball toss, a warrior's plight,
With squeals of joy, we launch, take flight!

In this dance, let worries slip,
As we embrace the cold's funny grip.
With every chill, and every cheer,
The muse of winter brings us near.

Reflections in a Glassy Veil

The mirror's surface gleams so bright,
A frozen dance, a slippery sight.
I tried to glide, but oh, what fun!
Ended up sprawled beneath the sun!

Icicles dangle like comical brats,
Waving at me, tipping their hats.
Snowflakes giggle, they winter waltz,
I lose my balance, it's all their faults!

Skates on my feet, I think I'm a pro,
But the ice has plans I do not know.
I tumble and twirl, in a frosty spree,
The snowman laughs; he's mocking me!

With every slip, I start to see,
Winter's a jester, and it laughs with glee.
In glassy veils of winter's art,
I become the joke, a frosty heart!

Splendor of the Wintry Light

The sun peeks through the frosty haze,
Making snowflakes sparkle in a daze.
I grab my mittens, oh what a sight,
A fashion disaster, but feeling bright!

The trees wear coats of shimmering white,
While squirrels play hide-and-seek in delight.
I join their chase, but to my surprise,
Face-plant in snow, oh, how time flies!

With throngs of flakes, a glittery scene,
I shout to the clouds, 'Let's start a routine!'
But each gust of wind sends me off track,
My dance moves, well, they're quite out of whack!

Yet here I stand, in winter's embrace,
Cracking up next to a snowman's face.
Laughter echoes in the frosty light,
In winter's grandeur, we reunite!

Beneath the Weight of Ice

Beneath the weight, the branches bow,
Like they're performing a wintery vow.
I waddle like a penguin, yes indeed,
With icy shoes, I'm quite the breed!

The pond's a sheet, so smooth and slick,
I challenge fate; let's try a trick.
With every twirl, I find my grace,
Lasting only seconds—I meet my base!

Frozen bubbles pop with a cheer,
"Join us," they say, "you've nothing to fear!"
So I plop down, and there I stay,
In a world of giggles, at end of day.

But the ice gives way, with a funny sound,
I bounce back up, feet off the ground.
With winter's weight upon my back,
I'm the punchline of this frosty act!

A Symphony of Shivering Stars

Under the night where the chill does play,
The stars are shivering in a joyful sway.
They chuckle softly, "Join us, my friend!"
But I'm too frozen; this shivering won't end!

The moon winks bright, wearing a crown,
While I'm stuck here, just spinning around.
I try to sing to the frosty skies,
But my voice turns into breathy sighs.

A snowball fight starting up on the hill,
I aim with precision, a terrible thrill.
The laughter erupts, as I slip with flair,
My clumsy retreat ends up waging a dare!

Yet here under stars, I join in the jest,
A symphony of laughter feels like the best.
Though frost nips at my nose, and the cold does tease,
In winter's laughter, my heart feels at ease!

Frost-Kissed Whispers Through the Pines

The pine trees wear their icy hats,
Squirrels slip and lose their chats,
Snowflakes tumble, what a sight,
Only to land and start a fight!

Balloons frozen in a tree,
A giggling ghost, just wait and see,
Frosty breath hangs in the air,
Who'd have thought a snowman could care?

The birds wear boots, they look so chic,
While snowballs fly, it's peak hide-and-seek,
Chasing shadows, slipping past,
Winter's fun, a joy that lasts!

So raise a glass of icy cheer,
To frosty things we hold so dear,
In nature's chaos, laughs abound,
Watch out for flakes, they've hit the ground!

The Still Dance of Winter's Breath

The flakes perform their swirling dance,
A frosty romance, oh what a chance,
Figured skaters strut with glee,
While penguins think, 'Look at me!'

Chatterboxes, chirp and tweet,
They huddle close, just to keep heat,
Hot cocoa spills on frosty toes,
What's colder, the drink or the snows?

Chattering teeth in the cold air,
Laughter echoes everywhere,
Frosty beards on giggly faces,
Winter's grip—so full of graces!

So let's pirouette and twirl, my mate,
In this frozen world, we create,
With every slip and frosty slide,
Laughter's the warmth we cannot hide!

Frosted Memories Beneath the Moon

Under moonlight, frosty beams,
Snowmen tell their silly dreams,
Chubby cheeks, a snowball's flight,
Pretend we're fighters in a snow fight!

Icicles hang like frozen swords,
Winter warriors, okay, we're bored,
But sliding down a snowy hill,
Who knew winter could bring such thrill?

Giggles wrap around the night,
As snowflakes dance, oh what a sight,
Frosty whispers in the breeze,
Teasing all with quiet tease!

So share a laugh, don't let it go,
In crazy fun, we steal the show,
The chilly air, a playful friend,
In these frosted moments, love transcends!

Glimmering Echoes of a Frozen Symphony

The winter's tune, a laugh out loud,
As snowflakes gather in a crowd,
A frosty choir, oh, what a sound,
With hip-hop howls that swirl around!

Gleeful giggles from every nook,
A snowball flies, oh, what a fluke,
In icy costumes, we prance and play,
While frosty shadows dance away!

A snowbank here, a skillful bounce,
Thumbs up for all who dare to pounce,
Frosty cheers as we glide and sway,
Winter's waltz turns night to day!

So join the fun in frosty glee,
Every chilly moment, pure esprit,
In glimmering echoes, we unite,
Creating laughter, oh what a sight!

A Symphony of Frost and Time

Snowflakes dance, oh what a sight,
Chilly noses, hearts feel light.
Frozen laughter fills the air,
Sipping hot cocoa without a care.

Snowmen wobble, carrots askew,
With goofy smiles, they greet you.
Yet the shovels, they plot and scheme,
Insulting our dreams, or so it seems.

Icicles dangle like teeth from a pout,
Nature's decor, there's no doubt.
But slip on ice, and it's quite the feat,
You'll be dancing in shoes of defeat.

So let's all twirl, sing songs of cheer,
Frost's cold grip, we hold so dear.
For with every slip, every frosty fall,
We find the funny in it all!

Beneath the Frosted Canopy

Beneath the trees, all glimmer and shine,
Chattering squirrels have lost all rhyme.
With puffs of snow, they leap and dive,
While we all wonder, how do they survive?

A frosty breeze gives cheeks a glow,
Our noses freeze, a rosy show.
Wearing mittens knitted with flair,
To lose one? Oh, please, simply unfair!

Penguins slide on their bellies with glee,
While we just wobble, oh woe is me!
Snowball fights turn faces to red,
As we hurl and dodge, it's fun, not dread.

The world feels like a snowy dream,
Posh and chic, or so it may seem.
But a snowflake here is not out of line,
When it lands on my nose, it's just divine!

Fragments of Icy Whispers

Icy leaves whisper secrets untold,
Under layers of frost, they wear coats bold.
As they giggle and shiver in the breeze,
They know winter's tricks, they know its tease.

Frosty patterns on windows appear,
Making lovely art that's oh-so-clear.
But then, we rush with cloth and grime,
To smudge it all away, oh what a crime!

A snowflake lands on a dog's wagging tail,
He shakes it off, like a furry hail.
Chasing shadows, they prance around,
While we sit laughing, joy knows no bound.

So let's toast to ice and cold's sense of wit,
With marshmallows floating in our cup, we'll sit.
And while frost makes the world twinkle and shine,
We'll cherish the laughter, each sparkly line!

Shivers Beneath a Starry Sky

Under the stars, with blankets we huddle,
Giggling softly, we play in the muddle.
When snowflakes tickle, it's quite the delight,
But shivers remind us that warmth feels just right.

A snowball flies, oh, what a surprise,
Right in the face, oh, how the laughter flies!
With rosy cheeks, and cold little toes,
This winter shenanigans, everyone knows!

The moon winks down, like it's in on our game,
As frosty the cat gives us all the blame.
She plots her revenge, eyes narrow with glee,
But a fuzzy warm lap is the place to be.

So raise your mugs beneath that bright dome,
Let's savor the season, no reason to roam.
For in giggles and shivers, we've truly found,
The magic of winter, all wrapped around!

The Allure of a Frigid Dawn

Snowflakes dance like tiny ballerinas,
While I slip on ice in fuzzy pajamas.
Hot cocoa's calling, but I'm stuck outside,
Chasing my hat as it takes for a ride.

Sunlight peeks through the frosty trees,
I stammer and mumble, "Please, oh please!"
But the squirrels just chuckle, their cheeks all round,
While I cartwheel awkwardly, falling to ground.

The morning is bright, but so are my cheeks,
Wishing for warmth as icy wind shrieks.
A snowman grins wide, it's all in good fun,
But I swear that he's laughing — the joke's never done.

I wave at the neighbors, who can't see my face,
Bundled so warmly, I'm losing my grace.
Yet, the joy of the chill brings a smile anew,
With each frosty step, I'm grateful for you!

Through the Frosted Lenses of Time

There once was a fellow with spectacles thin,
He fogged them while laughing, such a comical win!
As he squinted and frowned, the world turned to blur,
He bumped into snowmen — oh, what a stir!

The icicles dangle like teeth from the roof,
He laughed as he slipped, there's humor in goof!
With frostbitten toes, he trundled about,
Making snow angels, flopping about with a shout!

Old snowballs were gathered, to relive the past,
His memory faded, but the fun held steadfast.
Each toss brought a giggle, a moment sublime,
Through glasses now foggy, he's lost in the rhyme.

So here's to the moments wrapped tight in the freeze,
Where laughter's the warmth, and we do as we please.
With snowflakes a-drifting, let joy have its say,
In a world that grows chilly, we'll find a way!

Tranquil Moments in a Frozen World

When winter arrives, we bundle and play,
Wobbling like penguins, there's no other way.
A serenade of giggles fills crisp, frosty air,
As snowflakes land softly, without a cold care.

The kids build a fortress, a castle of fun,
Declaring it ruled by the Frosty Kingdom!
While parents sip cider, all cozy and warm,
We plot our next ambush — it's part of the charm.

With snowballs a-flinging, the laughter erupts,
As I find myself dodging while everyone jumps!
And just as I thought that I'd managed the score,
A sneaky young snowball — right in my core!

So we relish the freeze and the giggles it brings,
In this wintry wonderland, oh how joy sings!
Though tranquil it seems, chaos brews in delight,
With snowflakes like pillows, we frolic 'til night!

Crystal Dreams Under a Silver Sky

Beneath the bright stars, the world is aglow,
With icicles sparkling and frigid winds blow.
I dance with a snowman, his carrot nose bright,
And we twirl like madcaps, what a silly sight!

The moon chuckles softly, a witness to cheer,
As I trip on a snowdrift, give a shout that they hear.
The crystal dreams sparkle, a whimsical show,
While I roll in the snow, covered head to toe!

In the stillness of night, where the laughter unfolds,
A snowball fight starts, just as the moon scolds.
With cheeks rosy red, we forget all the rules,
As we waddle and giggle, like carefree fools.

So here's to the frosty, the cold and the fun,
In our magical kingdom, adventure's begun.
With crystal dreams dancing, and laughter in play,
We'll make every moment a whimsical day!